VANISHING HABITATS AND SPECIES

© Aladdin Books Ltd 2003

Designed and produced by
Aladdin Books Ltd
28 Percy Street
London W1T 2BZ

Revised and updated edition published in 2003
First published in Great Britain in 1993 by
Franklin Watts
96 Leonard Street
London EC2A 4XD

ISBN: 0 7496 4948 8

Design:	David West Children's Book Design
Designer:	Stephen Woosnam-Savage
Editors:	Fiona Robertson
	Jim Pipe
	Brian Hunter Smart
Picture research:	Emma Krikler
	Brian Hunter Smart
Illustrator:	Mike Saunders

A catalogue record for this book is available from the
British Library.

Printed in UAE

Environmental Disasters

VANISHING HABITATS AND SPECIES

JANE WALKER

FRANKLIN WATTS
LONDON • SYDNEY

CONTENTS

INTRODUCTION

In the past 100 years alone, human beings have destroyed almost half of the world's rainforests. We have filled in wetlands teeming with wildlife, and polluted coral reefs that are home to an astonishing variety of fish. We have poisoned the forests of Europe, and exhausted large parts of Africa's grasslands.

In the industrialised world, the growth of cities and towns, together with industrial and agricultural development, threaten many natural habitats. In the poorer developing countries, the desperate need for land, food and shelter leads to the destruction of valuable habitats and natural resources. Following the changes that human activities have made to so many natural habitats, animals struggle to survive as their homes and food supplies disappear.

We need to take action urgently to stop the trend of vanishing habitats, and to save those animal species that now face extinction.

HABITATS OF THE WORLD

"Habitat" is the name given to the home of a particular group of plants and animals. A natural habitat provides its living things with the conditions that they need to survive: air, water, food and shelter. A healthy habitat is, therefore, vital to the survival of the animal and plant species that live there. Over millions of years, many plants and animals have adapted so that they can survive in certain natural surroundings. For example, cactus plants can grow in hot, dry desert conditions because they can store water in their thick stems.

The world can be divided into various habitats. A single habitat can be home to thousands of different species. Together, they make up a huge web of life called an "ecosystem". All the plants and animals in an ecosystem depend on each other and on their habitat for survival. In a tropical rainforest, for example, monkeys and sloths depend on plants for their food. Many rainforest plants cannot reproduce without help from creatures such as birds and bats.

This map shows how the world can be divided into a number of natural habitats. One habitat can be distinguished from another by factors such as climate, rainfall, vegetation, rock and soil type, and local wildlife.

← The plants and animals that live in a desert must be able to survive for long periods without water. Many desert animals sleep underground during the day to avoid the scorching heat of the midday sun.

↓ Forests provide a natural habitat for thousands of different kinds of trees, plants, mammals, birds and insects.

KEY

■ Wetlands

■ Grasslands

■ Tropical forests

■ Deserts

■ Temperate forests

■ Mountains

■ Polar regions

← Only a few species of animals and plants can survive in the cold, harsh conditions of the world's polar regions – the Arctic and Antarctic. Plants have to grow very quickly during the short summers. Many animals hibernate or migrate to avoid the freezing temperatures of winter.

VANISHING HABITATS

Across the world, human activities are damaging and destroying natural habitats. This destruction can be witnessed in every corner of the globe, from the frozen Arctic in the north to the African grasslands in the south, and from Australia's Great Barrier Reef in the east to the Costa Rican wetlands in the west. As the world's population steadily increases, huge areas of natural habitat are cleared to provide land for housing and to grow food.

Many fragile and often unique habitats come under threat as developing countries try to catch up with the industrialised world. Dams are built across rivers and lakes to supply cheap and plentiful electricity. Coral reefs are destroyed by mining activities, or by the supply of coral souvenirs to the tourist industry. Tropical rainforests are cut down to provide timber, and over half the world's wetlands have been drained for development.

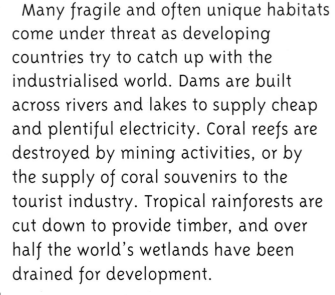

Forests are cut down and burned

↑ The plants and animals of the rainforest, like this one in Costa Rica, provide us with food, materials and even medicines. By threatening their survival, we risk losing a valuable storehouse of resources.

➤ The main illustration shows some of the ways in which human beings are destroying natural habitats.

More farmland is needed to grow crops

Roads and railways cut through undisturbed habitats

← The huge oil slick that appeared in the Persian Gulf toward the end of the 1991 Gulf War is just one example of the devastating effect of war on habitats. Crude oil poured into the calm waters of the Gulf after deliberate damage to Kuwaiti oil terminals and pipelines. Over 20,000 seabirds died as a result of the slick, and many other rare or endangered species were affected.

Dams are built across rivers to provide cheap hydroelectric power

Industrialised areas and large towns pollute the land, water and air around them

→ The damage to the land caused by open-cast mining is extensive. Such projects are usually accompanied by large-scale deforestation to clear land and provide fuel.

DESTROYING OUR FORESTS

Forests cover about 30 per cent of the Earth's land surface. They can be divided into three main types: tropical, deciduous and coniferous. Forests provide shelter for humans and animals, and are a valuable source of firewood, timber, food and raw materials such as rubber and oils. Yet the world's forests are being destroyed or damaged by humans at a terrifying rate.

By 1990, around 70 per cent of deciduous and coniferous forests in Europe were affected, though some are being replanted.

In tropical areas, forest destruction is far more severe. Heavy demand for tropical hardwoods such as teak has resulted in large-scale deforestation. Countries such as the Ivory Coast and Thailand have already lost over 80 per cent of their rainforests. Scientists estimate that nearly all rainforests could disappear by the year 2050.

← In countries such as Brazil vast forest areas are cleared to provide land for rearing cattle, sheep and goats. The land is soon exhausted due to overgrazing.

↓ Around one-fifth of the coniferous forests in Europe have been destroyed by acid rain. Acid rain is formed when moisture in the air mixes with polluting gases from industry and cars.

In Europe, extensive deforestation has reduced dramatically the habitat of the brown bear (below). These bears are now found only in remote locations, in parts of Scandinavia, Russia, northern Spain and the Italian Alps. Numbers of the Iberian wolf are also dangerously low.

Carbon dioxide
taken in

Moisture
taken in

← Trees play an important part in the water cycle. They help to control the world's climate and rainfall by taking in moisture and releasing it back into the atmosphere as water vapour.

They also release moisture into the surrounding soil and into nearby rivers and streams.

Forests help to control the world's atmosphere by taking in, or absorbing, carbon dioxide from the air. In turn, they produce oxygen, which all living things need to survive.

Oxygen
given
out

Moisture released
into the soil

Carbon dioxide
given out

→ Worldwide, rainforest destruction is estimated at 1 hectare per second, about equal to two football pitches, or 320,000 square kilometres per year – an area larger than Poland. The human activities that contribute to rainforest destruction include logging, cattle ranching, slash-and-burn agriculture and mining. After deforestation, there are no trees to protect the soil from being washed or blown away by rain and wind. The result is widespread soil erosion and frequent flooding in the valleys below the deforested areas.

Flooded
villages and
farmland

Evaporation
from the sea

Mud and silt from
deforested hillsides are
washed into nearby
rivers and seas

→ Around 25 per cent of the world's medicines come from rainforest plants. The Madagascar rosy periwinkle (right) is used to treat leukaemia. The genetic information and chemicals in rainforest plants and animals could be used to fight disease, but many are destroyed before their benefits can be discovered.

KEY
1 Harpy eagle   6 Three-toed sloth
2 Morpho butterfly 7 Hummingbird
3 Howler monkey   8 Jaguar
4 Toucan   9 Boa constrictor
5 Spider monkey   10 Tapir

← Around 1,800 species of bird and 3,000 species of fish live in the different layers of the Amazon rainforest. At least one plant or animal species may be disappearing every day.

↓ Huge roads such as the Trans-Amazon highway (below) are built through dense and unspoiled forest. They allow mining companies to reach the Amazon's rich supply of mineral resources. Opponents of the highway argue that the Amazon's resources would be better used for sustainable forestry and eco-tourism.

The Amazon habitat, home to such creatures as jaguars, is cut down to make way for cattle ranching and new roads. Giant anteaters are burned to death as their forest home is set on fire. Mercury, which is used to extract gold from the mines and rivers of the Rondonia goldfields, is released into the air as vapour. It falls into nearby rivers, killing fish and poisoning the water supply.

← Tribal peoples, like these Yagua Indians, also suffer from the continuing destruction. Their homes and land are taken away and many of the plants and animals on which they depend disappear. Contact with the outside world brings diseases like malaria, against which they have no resistance. More than 100 tribes have vanished from the Amazon in the past 100 years.

THE AMAZON

Almost half of the world's remaining tropical rainforest is found in the Amazon Basin in South America. The Amazon rainforest covers over 7 million square kilometres, and is home to several million species of plants and animals, making it one of the world's richest ecosystems.

Yet the destruction of this rainforest has been relentless, particularly since the early 1970s. The greatest cause of deforestation in the Amazon is land clearance. Fourteen per cent of the rainforest has already been cleared for cattle ranching. Mining and logging companies add to the rainforest's disappearance.

In 2001, the Brazilian Government announced a scheme to build over 10,000 kilometres of roads through the Amazon rainforest to encourage soya farming. Scientists predict that loggers and settlers attracted by the scheme will damage over 40 per cent more of the rainforest by 2020.

THE SPREADING DESERT

Grasslands can be found in tropical and temperate parts of the world, where low rainfall has prevented the growth of large numbers of trees. A combination of natural fires and large herds of grazing animals help to maintain natural grasslands.

Tropical grasslands support not only grazing animals, or herbivores, but also the carnivorous hunters that feed on them. Many wild animals migrate to other areas each year, allowing the grasslands to recover. However, growing numbers of domestic grazing animals, together with a gradual shrinking of grassland areas, mean that the vegetation is often eaten faster than it can regrow.

Another major threat is development, including roads. Breaking grassland up into small patches reduces its ability to maintain a wide variety of animal species.

← The African country of Mali (left) borders on the Sahel desert. More than 58 per cent of its land is desert and another 30 per cent is threatened. However, rapid population growth means that even the land on the desert edges is cultivated to grow food.

↑ Intensive farming in areas such as the Great Plains of the United States, above, has destroyed many temperate grasslands. The long-term use of chemicals prevents the soil from staying healthy. High-yielding crops, like wheat, take nutrients and water from the soil, making the land less fertile. Criss-crossing roads have also damaged the region, a vital breeding ground for birds.

Grassland is burned to encourage new shoots to grow

Heathlands

Large parts of the low-lying heath (level land having poor soil) in northern Europe have been developed for housing, farmland and leisure facilities like golf courses. Many of the wild animals that thrive in heath habitats are now in danger. Rare creatures that face extinction in Britain include the natterjack toad, the Dartford warbler, the sand lizard and the smooth snake.

Dartford warbler

Natterjack toad

Smooth snake

Cash crops replace local food crops

Overgrazing by herds of domestic animals

The soil becomes dusty and infertile

Trees are cut down for firewood

Rivers dry up because of the lack of rainfall

Domestic and wild animals compete for scarce water supplies

The deterioration of tropical grasslands is widespread in Africa. As the trees and grasses are stripped from the land, the topsoil becomes dry and dusty and is easily blown away. This process is known as desertification, and it occurs particularly in areas with very low rainfall, and at the edges of existing deserts.

DISAPPEARING WETLANDS

Wetlands are areas where land meets salt or fresh water, such as swamps, marshes and mangroves. They cover about 6 per cent of the Earth's surface and are found in places as varied as tropical Zambia and icy northern Canada.

Wetlands are a natural habitat for a rich variety of wildlife, particularly birds, fish and insects. They offer a plentiful food supply, which makes them an ideal place for fish to spawn and raise their young, and for birds to stop over and feed. The marshy vegetation acts as a buffer between the land and the sea, and protects against coastal erosion and flooding.

However, over 470 square kilometres of wetlands are still being destroyed worldwide each year, and many people remain unaware of their importance. They are drained and filled in to create homes, marinas and golf courses, or to make farmland. Waste from homes and factories pollutes other wetland areas, such as the delta area of the Danube River in Romania.

The destruction of tropical mangrove swamps is especially severe in Asia, where Malaysia, Pakistan and Thailand have each lost over 50 per cent of their wetlands.

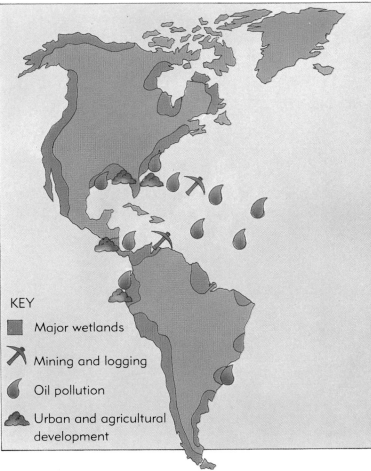

KEY

▨ Major wetlands

⛏ Mining and logging

💧 Oil pollution

🏚 Urban and agricultural development

↑ Coastal wetlands consist of mangrove swamps, tidal flats and saltwater marshes. Inland, freshwater wetlands include swamps, marshes, bogs, estuaries and floodplains. The world's major wetlands and the reasons for their disappearance are shown above.

← When part of the Wadden Sea in the Netherlands (left) was enclosed by a dam, it became a freshwater lake and the local bottle-nosed dolphins vanished.

← Water management schemes, such as dam construction and irrigation, reduce the flow of rivers. These mangrove swamps outside Lagos, Nigeria, are dying due to a drop in water levels.

Okavango Swamp

The Okavango Delta in Botswana, below, is one of the world's largest wetlands, clearly visible from space as an "eye" in the centre of southern Africa's last true wilderness. The Delta is home to many rare and endangered species, but it is now under serious threat from fires, over-hunting and ranching. The creation of huge cattle farms in Botswana has taken away much of the grazing land set aside for wildlife. Thousands of kilometres of fencing have been erected to protect the cattle against disease. The fences cut across the routes of the wild animals that migrate to the Okavango Delta during the dry season. Unable to reach vital water supplies, many wild animals die.

↑ Wetlands provide us with building materials, salt, crops such as rice, fish and shellfish. In Queensland, Australia (above), the tidal waters have been cut off from these mangrove swamps. The land will be used for development.

DESTRUCTION IN THE UNITED STATES

More than half of the 870,000 square kilometres of wetlands in the United States have already been destroyed. Each year, another 1,200 square kilometres disappear.

Although wetland drainage does provide good fertile farmland, in the long term wetlands are far more valuable in their natural state. They provide vital food supplies and spawning grounds for about 60 per cent of the fish around the US coastline. Hundreds of endangered bird species, such as the clapper rail and the least tern, and threatened plant species like salt-marsh bird's beak, also rely on their wetland habitat for survival.

On America's West Coast, 90 per cent of California's wetlands have fallen victim to the increasing demand to develop land for housing. On the East Coast, Chesapeake Bay, which lies near the cities of Baltimore and Washington, D.C., is famed throughout the world for its seafood, such as crabs and oysters. The widespread use of chemicals in agriculture is poisoning the Bay's waters. The pollution is killing the seagrasses and seaweeds on which the marine creatures feed.

Wetlands

Bogs

Prairie potholes

Cypress swamps

Floodplains

Salt marshes

UNITED STATES OF AMERICA

CALIFORNIA

The most serious destruction of US wetlands has occurred along the Gulf of Mexico coastline. In Florida, wetland drainage provides land for holiday and retirement homes. Inland, the floodplains of the Mississippi River are drained for agriculture.

GULF OF MEXICO

Wetlands trap large amounts of carbon in the decaying plant material that eventually becomes peat. When left undisturbed, this carbon is prevented from entering the atmosphere as carbon dioxide. However, wetland development and widespread peat cutting for fuel are releasing large amounts of carbon dioxide.

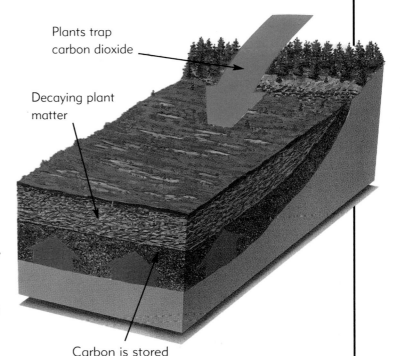

Plants trap carbon dioxide

Decaying plant matter

Carbon is stored

↑ Drainage of the Florida swamps, above, began in the mid-19th century. Today, half of the Everglades swamps have disappeared.

Chesapeake Bay

FLORIDA

No more songbirds

Many kinds of songbird, such as thrushes, orioles and warblers, nest in the United States and then migrate south for the winter, to the tropical forests of Central and South America. The destruction of these forests is leading to a steady decline in the numbers of songbirds found in the United States. Now, the disappearance of their wetland nesting grounds is making the problem even worse. Some species, such Bell's vireo (left), have almost disappeared altogether.

Coral is mined to obtain limestone for the building industry. This mining has caused widespread pollution off the coast of Kenya (left). Once coral has been destroyed, it takes years to regrow.

In the West Indies, the waste material from bauxite mining clouds the reef waters, which are usually clear. Many reef creatures are unable to breathe or feed properly, and, as a result, soon die.

The world's reefs

Coral reefs, such as the one below in the Red Sea, can be made up of hundreds of different kinds of coral. The reefs are home to marine animals such as the endangered loggerhead turtle, and dugongs. But reefs are being damaged by human activities in over 90 countries. Two-thirds of damage to coral in the Red Sea is caused by tourism.

The world's largest coral reef — the Great Barrier Reef — stretches for more than 3,000 kilometres off the coast of northeastern Australia. Much of the Reef has been protected since it was declared a Marine Park in 1983. Yet property developments and offshore oil exploration continue to damage the reef.

← On the Great Barrier Reef, the "crown of thorns" starfish feeds on coral polyps. The starfish is not affected by pollution, and its numbers are increasing dramatically.

↓ Sewage, silt, oil and chemical waste are just some of the forms of pollution which damage the world's coral reefs.

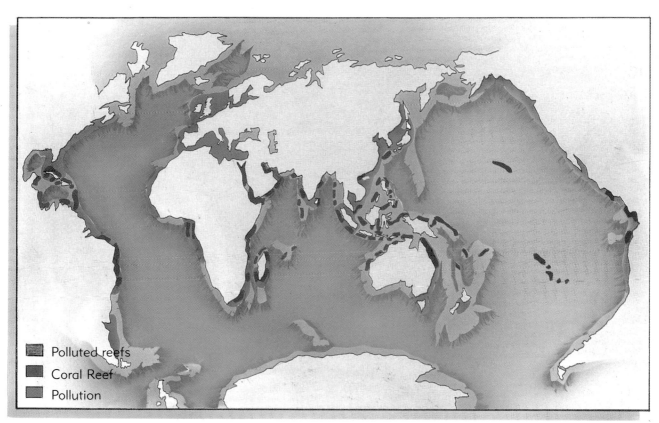

Polluted reefs
Coral Reef
Pollution

THREATENED CORAL REEFS

Coral reefs, the so-called rainforests of the ocean, are home to over 30 per cent of all known species of fish. They also help to protect coastlines from erosion by waves and from storm damage. Reefs are made up from the skeletons of millions of tiny living creatures, called coral polyps. The polyps need clear, warm water and plentiful sunlight to thrive. But across the world, coral reefs are under threat.

Global warming has caused many polyps to "bleach" and die. Mud and silt from deforested hillsides fill up nearby coastal waters and smother the coral. Human activity is also the likely cause for dozens of new infections found on coral since the 1980s. Reefs are also destroyed when coral souvenirs are collected for the tourist industry.

ANIMALS IN DANGER

Animal extinction is a natural process, with the weaker species that are unable to adapt to changing conditions continuously dying out. Earth also has a history of mass extinctions — the last occurred with the disappearance of the dinosaurs 65 million years ago. However, human beings have dramatically speeded up the natural rate of wildlife extinction.

  An estimated 1 per cent of all animal and plant species are vanishing from our planet every year, as we continue to damage and destroy their natural habitats. In the past 100 years, species such as the dusky seaside sparrow and more than one kind of Galapagos tortoise have already been wiped out completely. Thousands more animals are at risk from extinction, ranging from tiny rainforest termites to giant blue whales. Once extinct, these individual miracles of nature are gone for ever, along with their unique genetic code.

Mediterranean monk seal
The rare Mediterranean monk seal lives in the eastern Mediterranean Sea. Less than 500 of these seals remain, due to high levels of pollution in the Mediterranean, and disturbance from tourism.

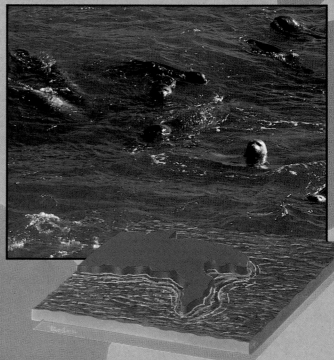

Jaguar and other big cats
Most big cats, such as jaguars (below), leopards and tigers, are under threat. This is mainly due to loss of habitat and hunting. Tigers may be extinct in the wild by 2025, and the wild population of Amur leopards is now reduced to between 20 and 30.

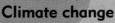

Climate change
The world's changing climate is now affecting many species. Shrinking sea-ice in the Arctic will reduce the numbers of ice algae. The algae forms the basis of the food chain, so fish, seals, birds, whales and polar bears will also be threatened. South of the Arctic Circle, many species are being forced to move north as habitats are affected by climate change.

Giant panda

There are fewer than 1,000 giant pandas left in the wild. Most live in the forested mountains of central China. Despite the creation of panda reserves by the Chinese government, the panda's natural habitat is shrinking as more land is used for housing and agriculture. Some pandas are left isolated in small pockets of forest, and are unable to breed with those from other areas.

African elephant

Elephants and rhinoceroses are both in great danger from habitat destruction. The woodlands and savanna that provide these big animals with both food and water are needed by humans for firewood and to grow crops.

Koala

Koalas, once found throughout Australia, are now a protected species because their forest habitat is burned down to clear land.

↑ In south-east Asia, over 100 dams have been planned for the Mekong River in the past 10 years, potentially affecting over 60 million people, who depend on the river for food, water and transport. The river also supports an enormous variety of freshwater fish.

➤ When the huge Aswan High Dam in Egypt was built in the 1960s, thousands of people lost their homes and lands. Many Nubian villages on the banks of the Nile had to be relocated.

The Sardar Sarovar Dam, India
Construction work is underway on India's Sardar Sarovar Dam, below. It is part of an irrigation and dam project along the Narmada River. About 240 villages will be flooded as a result of the scheme, making over 300,000 people homeless. The local animal population will also be threatened. Upstream the Bargi Dam has already flooded 27,000 hectares of fertile land and displaced 115,000 people.

PEOPLE ON THE MOVE

Habitat destruction creates problems for people, as well as wildlife. In many tropical countries, the desperate shortage of water for irrigation, combined with the need for cheap and plentiful electricity, results in large-scale water development schemes. A plan to build the massive Three Gorges Dam across China's Yangtze River could make over 2 million people homeless.

Deforestation in Central and South America and in South-East Asia has displaced millions of forest peoples, such as the Penan tribes in the Sarawak rainforest of Malaysia. Desertification also forces people to leave their homes to search for food and water. In the Sahel belt of Africa, farmers are forced to grow their crops at the desert edges, causing further damage to the land.

TAKING ACTION

To safeguard the world's natural habitats, we must prevent further destruction, as well as attempting to restore damaged habitats. Conservationists have targeted key areas, based on the number of species and the level of the threat. These include places with a unique wildlife, such as the Galapagos Islands, and large wilderness areas which are being destroyed at an alarming rate, such as the Amazon forests.

An immediate halt to the deforestation of tropical rainforests is an urgent priority. At the same time, we must create more timber plantations and encourage reforestation schemes. Soil conservation, and the use of more traditional methods of agriculture, can also help to protect the delicate tropical soils.

Controls on pollutants will reduce the damage these inflict on natural habitats. Pesticides are less harmful if they are made from natural substances found in plants.

Wildlife reserves
These help to protect those endangered species whose natural habitat has vanished.

→ **This illustration shows some of the agricultural methods that can be used to protect threatened habitats.**

Re-afforestation
Despite reforestation schemes, the rate at which the rainforests are being replanted is only about 10 per cent of the rate at which they are cut down.

← "Wildlife corridors" have been created to protect the threatened mountain gorillas living in the dense upland forests of Uganda, Zaire, left, and Rwanda. The corridors allow the animals to move safely between isolated areas.

→ In some poorer countries, the only means of earning money often involves habitat destruction, for example selling coral souvenirs to tourists (right). The Sri Lankan government banned reef mining in the 1980s, but paid compensation to thousands of people who had worked in the coral mining industry.

Agroforestry
Agroforestry is a method of farming where crops are grown alongside trees. The trees help to keep the soil fertile and protect against erosion.

Shelterbelts
Shelterbelts of trees can help to improve crop yields. They also prevent soil erosion and help the soil to retain moisture.

→ Many wetland plants, like the water hyacinth act as a kind of filter. They remove harmful substances such as lead and nickel from the water.

WHAT ARE WE DOING?

The United Nations set up its "Man and Biosphere" programme in 1974. It was designed to protect key environmental areas and has created more than 330 reserves worldwide. The 1992 Convention on Biological Diversity also places a duty on states to preserve habitats.

Wildlife organisations such as the World Wide Fund for Nature (WWF) and Conservation International have worked for many years to protect threatened habitats, while the Forest Stewardship Council (FSC) works with logging companies to help leave forests intact or give rare species a chance to recover.

Despite these efforts, hunting, pollution, economic development and climate change are continuing to take their toll on habitats worldwide. Habitat loss could threaten the lives of many millions of people, and 20 per cent of species may be extinct by 2030.

In the long term, the best way to protect these precious natural resources is for all of us to use less energy and produce less waste in our daily lives.

↓ This map shows how much land is protected in every country in the world. In total, around 5 per cent of the land is protected in some way, ranging from national parks and game reserves to highly protected wildlife sanctuaries.

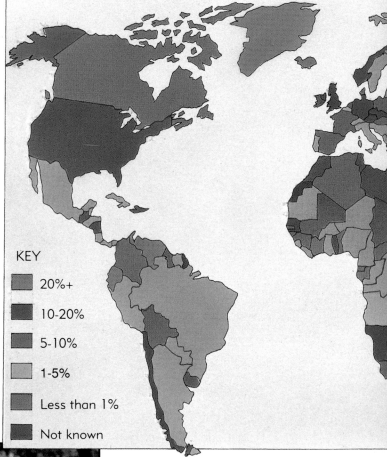

KEY
- 20%+
- 10-20%
- 5-10%
- 1-5%
- Less than 1%
- Not known

← In India, the Chipko Movement began as a protest against deforestation in the Himalayas. Local women hugged trees to stop them being cut down (the word chipko means "to hug" in Hindi). The movement now has an important environmental voice in India, and organises its own reforestation projects.

Project Tiger

Without the protection of special reserves, tigers would have disappeared from India. Under the Project Tiger scheme, started in 1972 by the WWF, 27 nature reserves have been created. Here, tigers can live and roam freely. However, though Project Tiger has helped to double the number of Bengal tigers in India from 1,800 in 1977 to over 4,000 today, they are still under threat from poaching.

↓ In northern Australia, plans to preserve the mangrove swamps have involved the local Aboriginal population. They harvest the swamps on a sustainable basis, so that no environmental damage takes place, and resources are not depleted for the future.

↑ On the island of Madagascar, off Africa's east coast, 22 National Parks and Reserves have been created to protect the island's threatened habitats and unique wildlife.

Strict reserve

Special reserve

Private reserve

FACT FILE

Rainforest cures

Ingredients for possible drugs have been found in more than 2,000 rainforest plants. A liana growing in the Amazon rainforest produces curare, which is used in a drug to relax muscles and to treat diseases like multiple sclerosis.

Grasslands around the world

The world's grasslands are commonly known by several different names. In tropical East Africa, the wide grassy plains are called savanna, while in Argentina they are known as pampas. In temperate regions, the term grasslands covers the steppes of Russia and Kazakhstan, the North American prairies and the veld of southern Africa.

Sharing the land

The fair distribution of land is a difficult problem to solve. In countries with rapid population growth, there is not enough land available to meet the demand for food. In South America, for example, less than 10 per cent of the population owns more than 90 per cent of agricultural land. The poorer majority of the population are unable to find land on which to grow their own food.

Global warming

The impact of global warming on threatened habitats and species will be profound. Polar bears will be stranded and starve as the ice retreats, and plants that grow in only a few areas may not survive rising temperatures. The world could lose thousands of natural species that have evolved over billions of years.

International treaties

1959 — Antarctic Treaty to promote international scientific cooperation in Antarctica. This sets aside Specially Protected Areas where important wildlife features are left undisturbed.

1971 — Ramsar Convention on Wetlands of International Importance. This protects against the development of wetland areas and the loss of plant and animal species, and encourages the careful use and management of wetlands by local people. By 2001, 1,073 sites were covered by the convention, totalling 81 million hectares of biodiverse or unique wetlands.

1973 — Convention on International Trade in Endangered Species of Wild Fauna and Flora (CITES). By 2002, over 150 states had signed the convention, which bans the international trade in rare and exotic animal and plant species.

1991 — Draft agreement by countries signing 1959 Antarctic Treaty to ban mining in Antarctica for the next 50 years.

1992 — Convention on Biological Diversity, signed by over 150 countries, requiring member states to conserve biodiversity.

1994 — The International Tropical Timber Agreement (ITTA). This promotes the sustainable management of tropical forests so that forests are largely left intact and tree species that are cut down are given a chance to recover.

1994 — Convention to Combat Desertification (CCD). This aims to combat desertification and to help fight severe droughts, particularly in Africa. By June 2002, 179 states had signed the convention.

2001 — Convention on Climate Change in Kyoto. After many years of negotiation a compromise agreement was reached by 180 countries, a significant first step towards concerted international action on global warming. However, the United States did not sign up to the treaty — even though it produces a quarter of the world's greenhouse emissions that cause global warming.

2001 — International Treaty on Plant Genetic Resources for Food and Agriculture. This treaty aims to protect the world's most important food and forage crops in an effort to safeguard global food security.

GLOSSARY

acid rain — rain that is made acidic when pollution from factories and cars mixes with moisture in the atmosphere. It can damage trees, soil and lakes.

agroforestry — a method of agriculture where trees and crops are grown together.

cash crop — any crop that is grown to be sold overseas rather than to be eaten by local people.

deforestation — the cutting down of large numbers of trees.

desertification — the spread of desert areas onto land that was once covered by grass and trees.

ecosystem — all the living things in a particular habitat, and the way in which they all affect each other.

erosion — the removal of soil or rocks by the action of wind and rain.

extinction — the total disappearance of a particular living thing from all areas of the world.

grassland — a type of natural habitat found in tropical and temperate parts of the world.

habitat — a place where certain animals and plants live and grow.

infertile — describes poor-quality soil in which crops can no longer grow.

irrigation — artificial watering of farmland in dry areas.

nutrient — a food substance that is taken in by plants and animals.

pesticide — a chemical product that is sprayed onto plants and crops to kill pests.

reforestation — the replanting of trees in an area where the forest has been destroyed.

silt — a mudlike material made out of very tiny pieces of rock. Silt is carried downstream by rivers and streams.

species — a group of living things that are very similar to each other.

sustainable — something that does not deplete resources or damage the environment.

temperate — describes something found in areas of the world that have warm summers, cold winters, and rain throughout the year.

tropical — describes something found in areas of the world that have high temperatures and heavy rainfall.

water cycle — the continuous movement of water backwards and forwards between the Earth's surface and the atmosphere: i.e. water evaporates, condenses and turns to rain.

wetland — a type of natural habitat where land is covered by either salty or fresh water.

INDEX

Photocredits

Abbreviations: l-left, r-right, b-bottom, t-top, c-centre, m-middle
Front cover l, 22bl — John Foxx Images. Front cover r — Digital Stock. Back cover, 4-5, 12b — Argentinian Embassy, London. 3, 24-25, 27t — Frank Spooner Pictures. 7t, 27b — Corel. 7m, 7b, 10 both, 14b, 16, 17bl, 20b, 21, 22mr, 23t — Bruce Coleman Ltd. 9 both, 17br, 23bl, 23bm, 26bl — Spectrum Colour Library. 13, 24b — Eye Ubiquitous. 14t, 17t, 25, 28, 29 — Panos Pictures. 19tl — Photodisc. 20t — Planet Earth Pictures.